A 40-DAY SPIRITUAL WORKOUT FOR CATHOLICS

A 40-DAY
SPIRITUAL
WORKOUT
FOR CATHOLICS

~BOB RICE~

SERVANT
BOOKS

PUBLISHED BY FRANCISCAN MEDIA
Cincinnati, Ohio

Scripture texts in this work are taken from the *New American Bible, revised edition* © 2010, 1991, 1986, 1970 Confraternity of Christian Doctrine, Washington, D.C., and are used by permission of the copyright owner. All Rights Reserved. No part of the *New American Bible* may be reproduced in any form without permission in writing from the copyright owner.

Quotes are taken from the English translation of the *Catechism of the Catholic Church* for the United States of America (indicated as CCC), 2nd ed. Copyright 1997 by United States Catholic Conference—Libreria Editrice Vaticana.

LIBRARY OF CONGRESS CATALOGING-IN-PUBLICATION DATA
Rice, Bob, 1972-
A 40-day spiritual workout for Catholics / Bob Rice.
    pages cm.
Includes bibliographical references (pages   ).
ISBN 978-1-61636-526-4 (alk. paper)
1. Spiritual life—Catholic Church. 2. Devotional literature. 3. Spiritual exercises. 4. Catholic Church—Prayers and devotions. I. Title. II. Title: Forty-day spiritual workout for Catholics.
BX2350.3.R535 2013
248—dc23
                              2012046115

ISBN 978-1-61636-526-4

Published by Servant Books, an imprint of Franciscan Media.
28 W. Liberty St.
Cincinnati, OH 45202
www.FranciscanMedia.org

Printed in the United States of America.
Printed on acid-free paper.
13 14 15 16 17 5 4 3 2 1

Contents

INTRODUCTION

Hello, my name is Bob. Think of me as your personal trainer for the next forty days. I'm thrilled that you're giving this spiritual workout a try, and I'm confident that you will grow stronger in Christ because of it. But first let's cover some of the W's of this spiritual workout:

Who: *You.* I know that sounds obvious, but it's an important point. *Nobody can be holy for you.* You can be a part of the most amazing spiritual community ever (and I hope you are!), but that doesn't mean you are a follower of Jesus Christ. We need to pray as a community, but we also need to learn how to pray individually.

Praying with a community encourages you to pray on your own; praying on your own makes you more eager to pray with a community. It's like running with both feet!

But it's not just you. It's also *Him*—specifically, the Holy Spirit. Unlike a physical workout where the focus is on your own effort, a spiritual workout is about opening yourself up to the power and love of God. You can't do this on your own.

You don't even know how to speak God's language! But St. Paul tells us, "The Spirit too comes to the aid of our weakness; for we do not know how to pray as we ought, but the Spirit itself intercedes with inexpressible groanings" (Romans 8:26). The Spirit dwells within us and teaches us how to pray! So call on the Holy Spirit, and pray with Him!

What: What is prayer? It's a word we often hear but rarely understand. The *Catechism of the Catholic Church* (which is where all the teaching about prayer in this spiritual workout comes from) says that prayer is "a vital and personal relationship with the living and true God" (CCC, 2558). St. Thérèse of Lisieux said it beautifully: "For me, prayer is a surge of the heart; it is a simple look turned toward heaven, it is a cry of recognition and of love, embracing both trial and joy."

Prayer isn't a formula or an empty ritual. It's a friendship. It's a relationship. That means it's a dialogue of love by which people in love talk to each other. The God who loves you and made you has a lot to share with you. Will you listen? How will you respond? This is what prayer is about. And this is what the spiritual workout is about.

Why: Why pray? Because you're thirsty. Like the woman at the well, you are desperate for "living water" (John 4:11, 15).

But you know what? God is thirsty too. He thirsts for us. "Whether we realize it or not, prayer is the encounter of God's thirst with ours. God thirsts that we may thirst for him" (*CCC*, 2560; see St. Augustine, *De diversis quaestionibus octoginta tribus* 64, 4: PL 40, 56).

Prayer isn't optional for Christians. *It's what we do*. Imagine meeting someone who says she is a runner but doesn't like to run. Or a swimmer who doesn't ever go into the water. You'd tell those people they aren't who they say they are. Runners *run*. Swimmers *swim*. Christians *pray*.

A Christian who doesn't pray is not a Christian.

St. Paul tells us, "Pray without ceasing" (1 Thessalonians 5:17). There are many ways to pray. Prayer finds its perfect expression in the Mass. Serving the poor, caring for the needy, and all the works of mercy are prayer. Whether we're asking God for help before a test, saying grace before meals, or looking at the beauty of creation and whispering, "God, I love you"—these are all ways that we live out lives of prayer.

This *40-Day Spiritual Workout* is to help train you in focused periods of personal prayer. Scripture tells us that Jesus frequently went off to pray by Himself (see Matthew 14:23; Mark 1:35; Luke 5:16). That is our model for this prayer time. Though we should pray throughout the day, it's vital that we set aside some time in our day solely for Him.

Where: It's true that you can pray wherever you are, but some places are more suitable than others. If you were going to do a physical workout, you might go to a gym or move a table in your living room to give yourself space. The same is true with a spiritual workout.

Pray at church in front of the tabernacle, or set aside a place in your room for prayer. It might be a small place—when I was a teen, I had a corner of a table where I had a candle, a Bible, and a picture of Jesus. Your prayer will be more effective if you have a good place to do it.

When: Herein lies the greatest challenge of this spiritual workout. When should you pray?

Many times people lament, "I don't have time to pray!" But that's not true. We make time for things that are important to us. How is it that we don't have time for prayer, but we have time for other things, like watching videos and using Facebook?

The answer is that watching videos and using Facebook and other kinds of media and social communication are *easy*. They require little or no effort. Prayer, on the other hand, is a challenge. It takes commitment, dedication, and perseverance.

So you have to *make time* to pray. That means you might have to sacrifice something in your busy schedule. What will that be? Time on the Internet? Time in bed?

Don't be foolish enough to think that you will just "find time" to pray. Before you go to bed, decide when you are going to pray the next day.

You might wonder why this workout lasts for forty days. In the Bible, forty is a significant number. When God cleansed the world from those who rebelled against Him, He put Noah on the ark for forty days. When He wanted to transform the hearts of the Hebrews from those of Egyptian slaves to those of the people of God, He led them through the wilderness for forty years. When Jesus began His public ministry, He fasted in the desert for forty days to overcome Satan's temptations. And after He rose from the dead, Jesus spent forty days with His apostles, preparing them for the coming of the Holy Spirit and the birth of the Church, before He ascended into heaven.

So whenever God wants to bring about major transformation, He takes forty days—or years—to do it. Since creating a Bible study for forty years would be a lot of work, let's just stick with forty days.

A 40-Day Spiritual Workout for Catholics is a daily Scripture reflection to bring about deeper transformation and conversion in your life. Perhaps you're coming off a retreat or a conference, or maybe you want to jump-start your soul and grow in your faith. Maybe you want to know a more effective way to pray, or you desire to have a better understanding of what it means to be Catholic. Whatever the reason, this spiritual workout will help you grow stronger in your faith and lead you to deeper intimacy with Jesus Christ.

Throughout these forty days I'll be adding steps to your spiritual workout, just as a physical trainer intensifies a regimen. Two things you'll start out with are "hydration" and reflection. Every workout needs to begin with adequate hydration: In a physical workout it's plenty of water and other fluids; in a spiritual workout it's the Word of God. I'll give you a Scripture passage or passages each day to reflect on. Think of them as water for the soul.

So let's begin!

How to Read the Bible

Maybe you've never cracked open a Bible before. I know it looks big, and it can be intimidating, but you'll get comfortable with it in no time.

Every day you are going to read a few verses in different places of the Bible. So if I tell you to read John 3:16, you'll go to the Gospel of John (which you can find in the table of contents in your Bible), then go to the third chapter, and read the sixteenth verse. I've tried to use Scripture verses that are spread throughout the Bible, so sometimes you'll have to do some searching. Think of it as a fun treasure hunt to find the greatest treasure of all: the Word of God!

If you don't own a Bible, it's worth getting! No other book has changed the world like the Bible. There's a popular saying that B.I.B.L.E. stands for "Basic Instructions Before Leaving Earth." But it's more than just a "how to" book—it's God's personal love letter to you.

There are a lot of translations out there (the Bible was originally written in Hebrew and Greek), such as the *New American Bible*, the *Revised Standard Version*, the *New Jerusalem Bible*, and so on. Make sure you get a Catholic translation, because there are some books in our Scriptures that our Protestant brothers and sisters don't include. The translation I use for this book is the *New American Bible*, because that is the translation read at Mass. (You can read this translation on the U.S. Catholic bishops' website, www.usccb.org.)

There's an app for this!

On the go? Forget your book? Don't worry—we've got you covered. If you have an iPhone, go to the app store and look for "40-Day Spiritual Workout." If you're online, go to Steubenville. org to get e-mails for each day.

GOD'S LOVE FOR YOU

● **Hydration:**   JOHN 3:16 | WISDOM 11:24–26 | ROMANS 5:8
● **Reflection:**   God loves each of us as if there were only one of us. —*St. Augustine*

A couple I know, upon finding out they were pregnant, prepared their house for the new arrival. They took a room that was used for storage and made it into a baby room. They even painted it to look like the inside of a Dr. Seuss book! The father spent every weekend making that room as beautiful as it could be. It became a symbol of love from a father to his future son.

In the biblical story of creation in the book of Genesis, God created a "room" for us. He made a paradise. Then he made us and put us in the middle of that paradise. After creating the sea, sun, stars, and so on, God said, "It is good." But after creating us He said, "It is *very* good." Wow.

When I proposed to my wife, I pledged to live my entire life with her. I didn't want to love her from afar—I wanted to spend every moment with her. I wanted a relationship with her, and I asked her to commit to a relationship with me. Upon seeing my great love for her, Jennifer had to respond. You can't just be proposed to and try to change the subject. I asked, waited, and rejoiced as she broke into tears and said, "Yes!"

All of creation is crying out to you now as the Creator of the universe bows down and asks you to be in a relationship with Him. Such an act of love demands your response. He has asked and is waiting. And as you say yes, a great celebration begins.

As you begin this journey of love, meditate upon the Bible verses and allow yourself to be overwhelmed by the love that God has for you. And if you haven't already said yes to God in your heart, do so. Being born into a Catholic family isn't what makes you Catholic. Being Catholic, following Christ, is a decision of the heart. It is a relationship with Love Himself and a commitment to be faithful to the One who has faith in you.

WHAT IS SIN?

● **Hydration:** GENESIS 3:4–6

● **Reflection:** Man, tempted by the devil, let his trust in his creator die in his heart and, abusing his freedom, disobeyed God's command. This is what man's first sin consisted of. All subsequent sin would be disobedience toward God and lack of trust in his goodness. —CCC, *397; see Genesis 3:1–11; Romans 5:19*

Our reading in Genesis 3 can make us wonder about God. If God is all-knowing, why did He put the tree there in the first place? Didn't He know Adam and Eve would eat from it? If God is all-present, where was He when they were tempted? If God is all-powerful, why did He let this happen? And what's so bad about eating from "the tree of knowledge of good and evil" (Genesis 2:17)?

Well, Adam and Eve already knew what was good and what was evil, because they were created in the image of God. So what did the fruit offer? Listen to the words of the serpent: "You will be like gods, who know good and evil" (Genesis 3:5). The tree didn't offer the ability to *see* what was good and what was evil. It gave the ability to *choose* what was good and what was evil.

In other words, things that God says are wrong, we can say are right. Things that God asks of us, we can deny. We start to justify things and convince ourselves that we are right and God is wrong. Adolf Hitler murdered millions of Jews, Catholics, and others, yet biographers say he never felt guilty. Why? Because he convinced himself that what he was doing was right. In sin we decide to become our own gods. When we ignore the Creator and follow our own selfish desires, we end up hurting ourselves. God can live without us, but we can't live without God.

God wants a relationship with us. A real love relationship can't be forced; it has to be chosen. God had to offer us a choice, that is, *free will*. That's why the tree was in the garden. That's why He allowed Adam and Eve to eat from it. He allows us to freely choose what we want, in the hopes that we will freely choose Him.

Pray for an awareness of sin in your life, and offer those sins up to God. It is only when we say we're sorry that we can hear the words, "I forgive you." And if you haven't gone to confession recently, you should go receive the wonderful graces offered to you in this sacrament.

DAY 3

THE POWER OF THE CROSS

● **Hydration:** 1 PETER 2:24–25 | ROMANS 6:23 | JOHN 3:16
● **Reflection:** Apart from the cross, there is no other ladder by which we may get to heaven. —*St. Rose of Lima*

Many people assume they will get to heaven but don't follow God in their daily lives. They seem to think that because God is good, He won't send people to hell. For that matter, if God is good, how can a place like hell even exist? The surprising answer is that hell exists *because* God is good. He is so good that He doesn't force Himself on anyone.

Heaven isn't just a place we go. It's a wedding feast where we experience ultimate intimacy with Love Himself: God. But if we don't want to follow God in this short life, why would He think we'd want to be with Him forever? I wouldn't marry a girl whom I had never dated or even wanted to talk to. So God, in His love, allows a place where those who don't want Him in their lives can go. That place is called hell. It's not so much a place God sends people to; it's a place they send themselves by the lives they live. Hell is the ultimate separation from God.

But that's not where God wants us to be. Sin brought death and separation from God into the world. Jesus came into this world to die for us and bring us once again into union with Him. Jesus' death on the cross and His resurrection from the dead offer us a new life. When He uttered the words "It is finished," He was referring to the triumph over our sins, a triumph promised all the way back in Genesis 3:15.

Through Christ there is nothing that can't be forgiven. And only Christ's sacrifice for us can pay the debt we owe to God (and each other) for our sins. By accepting Christ's sacrifice for us, we can be part of God's family again—in this life and in the next.

Take time to pray before a crucifix, and thank Jesus for his love. Reflect on the beauty of John 3:16, and commit the verse to memory. It's the most perfect statement of God's love for us.

WHO IS JESUS?

Hydration: JOHN 1:1, 14 | COLOSSIANS 1:15–20 | JOHN 20:27–28

Reflection: A man who was merely a man and said the kind of things Jesus said would not be a great moral teacher. He would either be a lunatic on a level with the man who says he is a poached egg—or else he would be the Devil of Hell. You must make your choice. Either this man was, and is, the Son of God: or else a madman or something worse. —*C.S. Lewis*

It can be safely said that no other person in human history has had the impact that Jesus did. There have been more books written, more songs sung, and more buildings built in His name than anyone else. The world has not been the same since His birth in Bethlehem—historians even renamed *time* after Him. But who is He?

The Bible has a simple answer: Jesus is God.

In the beginning of the Gospel of John, we read about how the Second Person of the Trinity, the Word that created the universe, became flesh and dwelt among us (see John 1:14). He was named Jesus, which means "God saves." He always existed in God and always was God, but in coming to earth He became fully man while remaining fully God. He was not half God, half man. He was not God in a human suit. He took on our humanity. He wept, He was tempted, He suffered, and He died. Jesus was like us in all things but sin. He was true God and true man.

Jesus revealed to us that God is the Father, the Son (Jesus), and the Holy Spirit. Each Person of the Trinity is individual and unique, yet They are all one. Throughout the Gospels we see Them work together for our salvation. Jesus often prayed to the Father for strength and guidance, and He worked in the power of the Holy Spirit.

Jesus is the "image of the invisible God" (Colossians 1:15). In the Old Testament God forbade the Israelites to create images of Him. But now we can "see" who He is!

Isn't it amazing that our God took on our flesh? That He chose to be born in poverty and die in suffering so that we could know His love and be reconciled to Him? Take some time to think about this. He wants to be more than an example, a teacher, or a friend. Jesus is God. And He wants to be *your* God, because He loves you.

HOW TO DRINK LIVING WATER

● **Hydration:**   JOHN 4:13–14 | ISAIAH 55:1 | 2 TIMOTHY
              3:16–17
● **Reflection:**   God is a spring of living water which flows
              unceasingly into the hearts of those who pray.
                                    —*St. Louis De Montfort*

Hydration is important in any kind of exercise. There was a
movie many years ago that featured a man who had "a drinking
problem." Every time he poured himself a drink, he opened his
mouth and splashed the drink on his face!

Silly as that sounds, many times we do that with God's Word.
We let the living water of God splash our face, but we don't take
time to drink it in and let it change our lives. Another problem
with hydration in exercise is drinking too much too fast. The
body can't deal with the water it's receiving, and the water ends

up filling the stomach and leaving the drinker bloated and sick. The "living water" we are drinking in our workout is Sacred Scripture. Are you reading it too lightly (splashing the water on your face), or are you trying to chug it down (reading it all quickly without much thought)?

To make your spiritual workout effective, you need time to *meditate* on God's Word. Sometimes when we hear the word *meditate*, we think of Eastern mysticism. But to meditate simply means to approach God's word using our imagination, thought, emotion, and desire. So don't rush through the Scriptures. Unlike physical workouts, where you might try to do the same activity faster and faster, the goal here is to *take it slow*. Use your imagination. Think about what God is saying. Let His words speak to you.

Unlike our Protestant brothers and sisters, who believe that Scripture is the *only* authority, we Catholics believe that the word of God is in more than just the Bible. We also believe in Tradition—the teaching of the apostles passed down to us today. Scripture and Tradition aren't two different things. Scripture came *from* Tradition—that's where we got the Bible in the first place! We see Tradition fully alive in the Mass and in the sacraments.

In the Mass we start with Scripture and end with the Sacrament; that's the way it should be in our lives, too. Reflecting on Scripture in private should prepare us to receive the sacraments, especially the Eucharist. And receiving the sacraments should open our hearts more for reading God's words in Sacred Scripture.

To find out more, check out the *Catechism of the Catholic Church*, 105–108, 2705–2708.

THE PERFECT PRAYER

Hydration: MATTHEW 6:9–13

Reflection: The Lord's Prayer is the most perfect of prayers.... In it we ask, not only for all the things we can rightly desire, but also in the sequence that they should be desired. This prayer not only teaches us to ask for things, but also in what order we should desire them.
—*St. Thomas Aquinas*

When the disciples asked Jesus how to pray, said he taught them the Our Father (or the Lord's Prayer). This prayer is perfect, not only because of the simplicity of its words but also because of what it represents. I bet you've heard or prayed the Our Father a thousand times. But do you know what it is about?

Our Father, who art in heaven: Not "my Father," as if God is only for the individual. God is *our* Father, meaning we not only have an amazing dad, but we are all part of an incredible family! The phrase "who art in heaven" acknowledges God's glory in all eternity.

Hallowed be Thy name: We live in a culture that uses the name of God a lot but usually not for sacred things! The word *hallow* in this context is "to recognize as holy." We want the world to know that God's name is holy.

Thy kingdom come: Did you know you were praying for the end of the world? We not only pray for the future but also for today, that His kingdom will continue to grow until He comes again.

Thy will be done: We want what He wants, knowing that His will is the best for us and for the world.

Give us this day our daily bread: Bread refers not only to our earthly nourishment but also to our eternal nourishment: Jesus is the Bread of Life. We ask for what we need today for our bodies and our souls.

Forgive us our trespasses as we forgive those who trespass against us: Notice the phrase "as we forgive." We're not just asking for mercy; we're also expressing mercy to others. This is necessary if we are to hope for mercy from God (see Matthew 18:23–35).

Lead us not into temptation: Though God will give us opportunities to prove our faith, He never tempts us with sin, like the devil does. We ask to remain strong in times of temptation so that, by His grace, we will not fall into sin.

Deliver us from evil: The "evil" referred to here is the devil. This final petition asks God to show His victory over the devil and save His children (also known as *us*).

It's amazing how much is packed into this "perfect" prayer! But the words only make a difference if we mean them. So as a way to "cool down" after your workout, pray the Our Father every day. But don't speed through it. Take some time to think about what the words mean. There is no better spiritual workout than that.

● **Cool Down:** Pray an Our Father.

STRETCHING

● **Hydration:** EPHESIANS 1:3 | PSALM 134
● **Reflection:** We bless him for having blessed us.
—*CCC, 2627; see Ephesians 1:3–14; 2 Corinthians 1:3–7; 1 Peter 1:3–9*

Every good physical workout begins with stretching. It loosens cramped muscles and increases flexibility so that exercise can be more effective. What's true for the body is true for the soul. At the beginning of a spiritual workout, we need to stretch our souls so we can be more open to receiving God's grace.

How do we do that? It's called the prayer of blessing.

First, we bless God. Sounds weird, right? Why would God want us to bless *Him*? Think of "blessing" as "giving permission."

When we bless God, we give Him permission to work in our lives—we say yes to Him.

Second, God blesses us. He showers us with His grace and His love. The more we open ourselves to Him, the more He can fill us with His Holy Spirit.

This prayer of blessing should lead us to a moment of adoration, in which we are silent before God and contemplate how amazing it is that He wants to spend time with us. Jesus called us His friends, but He's not like our neighbor down the street. He is the GOD OF THE UNIVERSE. And we are, well, *us*. In the eyes of the world, we are only insignificant specks in the dust of time. But in the eyes of God's love, we are *invaluable*. Understanding the truth of God's majesty and our own smallness is called *humility*, and it's an essential attitude of prayer.

From now on, start your spiritual workouts with a good stretch by spending a few minutes with blessing and adoration. It will make your reflections on Scripture that much better.

And here's something to bless God for: You've finished the first week of the workout! Great job! Have a cookie or some other kind of treat today to celebrate.

PS: Scripture talks a lot about lifting up your hands to bless God. Feel free to do that during this time of prayer. It's a cool way to connect your body with what you're doing in your soul. If you want to read more about prayer of blessing and adoration, check out the *Catechism of the Catholic Church*, 2626–2628.

● **Cool Down:** Pray an Our Father.

DAY 8

THE MEANING OF LIFE

● **Stretch:** Prayers of blessing and adoration.

● **Hydration:** MATTHEW 6:25, 33 | JOHN 10:10 | JEREMIAH 29:11

● **Reflection:** Q: Why did God make you?

A: God made me to know Him, to love Him, and to serve Him in this world, and to be happy with him in the next. —*Baltimore Catechism*

Maybe you have come to a place in your life where you're asking, "What's the point?" You work hard in high school to get to college. You work in college to get a job. You get a job so you can pay bills. Then you die. It's like the bumper sticker: "Birth, School, Work, Death." Sounds exciting, doesn't it?

There is no purpose in life without our Creator. A person trying to find meaning in life without God is like a television trying to find work without being plugged in. It could be a table or a doorstop, but it would never live up to the fullness of what it was created to be.

We were created for God. It's that simple. This life is an extremely brief time (especially compared to eternity) in which we have the chance to freely choose Christ. It's not just a "suffer now and get paid later" kind of deal. Jesus offers life in abundance. The kingdom of God begins here!

We celebrate it at every Mass. We experience it in the deep love we give and receive from others. We can taste a small bit of heaven on earth. This is what makes life meaningful.

Does this mean that everything will be great from here on out? No. Christianity does not offer a life free of suffering. But from the cross we see that our suffering does not need to end in death; it can bring new life. This is the hope God offers us, which the world cannot give.

Think about the things you spend your time on. Do they bring you or others closer to God? If meaningless things are getting in the way of meaningful ones, maybe you should cut them out of your life. Think about how you can spend your time on this earth so as to build up treasures in heaven.

● **Cool Down:** Pray an Our Father.

DAY 9

WHO YOU REALLY ARE

● **Stretch:** Prayers of blessing and adoration.
● **Hydration:** 1 JOHN 3:1 | ROMANS 8:14–15 | ISAIAH 64:7
● **Reflection:** *We are not the sum of our weaknesses and failures;* we are the sum of the Father's love for us and our real capacity to become the image of his Son. —*Blessed Pope John Paul II*

One of the most amazing days of my life was the day I met my son Joseph. Unlike our other children, Joseph was adopted from Haiti when he was two years old.

Before Joseph arrived I was worried. *Would I love him as much as I love my other kids?* My other kids were born, and I fell in love. It just happened. But what about a child who came from a different place and had different biological parents?

My wife and I had to wait for hours at Miami International Airport before Joseph finally arrived. And then I saw him! Tears ran down my face, and my heart cried out: *That is my son!* It didn't matter that he had different color skin and came from different parents. I loved him as my own from the moment I laid eyes on him.

And then it hit me: *That is how God the Father loves us.*

We are all adopted children in God's family. God had no reason to love us. And yet He *chose* to love us. He chose to love *you*.

I've given Joseph everything I have: my love, my support, even my last name. But if you looked at a picture of the Rice family and played the game "One of These Things Is Not Like the Others," it wouldn't take you long to spot the kid with brown skin and brown eyes among the pale Irish people. That's because I can't give him my DNA.

This is where the adoption of God is different. At our baptism God infused His spiritual DNA into our souls. The blood of Christ not only washes us clean but transforms us into children of God! We are sons and daughters of the living God!

In this life we are given many titles. The following apply to me: son, father, husband, writer, speaker, musician, and professor. Your titles will be different. But at the end of our lives, all those titles fade except for one: son or daughter of God. Never let other "titles" compete with your true identity. You are a son or daughter of God Almighty. When you look at the cross, reflect on how much God went through to bring you into His family.

● **Cool Down:** Pray an Our Father.

STAY FOCUSED!

● **Stretch:**   Prayers of blessing and adoration.
● **Hydration:**   Matthew 6:19–21 | Psalm 27:7–8
● **Reflection:** The habitual difficulty in prayer is *distraction*.... To set about hunting down distractions would be to fall into their trap, when all that is necessary is to turn back to our heart. —CCC, 2729

Distracted yet?

One of the biggest difficulties in prayer is distraction. We begin by praying to God but end up thinking about a show that we just saw on TV or a situation with a friend. Or we fantasize about living a different life. Don't worry, that happens to everybody. And it's not worth focusing on the distractions, because that just makes us even *more* distracted.

There is an opportunity for grace when we are distracted. The *Catechism* tells us "a distraction reveals to us what we are attached to" (CCC, 2729). Even though many of us desire our hearts to be totally committed to the Lord, the things we think about reveal the other things that are competing for our hearts.

Think about your distractions and why they are attractive to you. We might have different fantasies, but they are usually driven by the same motivation. Do we wish we were more popular? More successful? More attractive? Those things are the "treasures" that Jesus warns about in Matthew 6, but we should be storing our treasures in heaven. The next time you are distracted, ask the Lord what is at the heart of that distraction. Pray for grace to turn your heart back to God.

And don't stress about the distractions. We *all* face them in prayer. Just keep bringing your attention back to Him. As St. Francis de Sales wrote, even if you spend your entire prayer time offering your distractions back to him, your prayer will be worthwhile.

If you want to read more about how to deal with distractions in prayer, check out the *Catechism of the Catholic Church*, 2729–2730.

● **Cool Down:** Pray an Our Father.

FAITH (IN ACTION)

- **Stretch:** Prayers of blessing and adoration.
- **Hydration:** JAMES 2:14–17 | 2 CORINTHIANS 5:7 | LUKE 17:5–6
- **Reflection:** Faith is to believe what you do not see; the reward of this faith is to see what you believe. —*St. Augustine*

Our society thinks that faith only refers to what we believe, but faith is more than just an intellectual exercise. It refers not just to what we believe but also to how we live.

Faith inspires action. For example, if I had faith that I knew the winning lottery numbers, but that faith didn't inspire me to buy a ticket, what good would it do me? What we believe should affect how we live.

Learning about our faith should inspire us to live our faith. The more you learn about God, the more your life will change. Can you see areas in your life that are changing? That is because faith is at work in you. Maybe you are not giving in to sin as easily. Maybe you are being kinder to people. Or maybe you are seeing life in a whole new way.

Those are signs of a growing faith. Faith is like a sixth sense— it allows us to see beyond what our other senses tell us. It doesn't deny our other senses; it enhances them. Faith allows us to see hidden realities that are truly present, so we can "walk by faith, not by sight" (2 Corinthians 5:7). For example, faith enables us to see God in the Eucharist. It also lets us see God in the poor and suffering.

Faith is a virtue. Virtues are like spiritual muscles: The more we work them, the stronger they get. We must always seek an active faith—one that is active in learning and active in living.

What are some ways you can put your faith into action?

● **Cool Down:** Pray an Our Father.

EYES ON THE PRIZE

Stretch: Prayers of blessing and adoration.

Hydration: PHILIPPIANS 3:13–14 | HEBREWS 12:1–2
ROMANS 8:24–25

Reflection: At the time of temptation think of the love
that awaits you in heaven: foster the virtue of
hope. —*St. Josemaría Escrivá*

In 1998 U.S. fifteen-year-old figure skater Tara Lipinski became
the youngest Olympian ever to win a gold medal. In a TV
interview she said that when she was six years old, she used to
practice receiving the gold medal. She always knew what she
wanted. She kept her eyes on the prize.

In running the race of faith, we need to keep our eyes on our
prize: eternal salvation and glory in Jesus Christ. This is known
as the virtue of hope.

In today's world *hope* is a wishy-washy term. We say, "I hope I pass this test," or, "I hope this person calls me." What we mean is that we don't think it will happen. In Scripture, though, hope is more than a wish. Hope refers to the belief that *we will* be saved. Hope is knowing the eternal glory that awaits those who have been faithful to Christ. It is definite. It is confident.

Many people confuse faith with hope. Faith refers to our living out what we believe; it's our daily steps. Hope is the reason we run. We must fix our eyes on Jesus if we want to win this race (see Hebrews 12:2). We must continually remind ourselves of the glory that awaits us in heaven.

Imagine this: You close your eyes for the last time on this earth, and when you open them again, you are in a different place. It is the most beautiful place you have ever seen. Before you is the finish line. As you head toward it, you see deceased family members calling your name and shouting for joy. You see angels and saints clapping and shouting louder and louder. Behind the finish line you see Jesus, with a huge smile and His arms outstretched. As you break through the finish line into his arms, all of creation erupts in song. He then puts you on a pedestal and, In front of all creation, he places on your head the crown of life. It is the most incredible moment you will ever experience. And it will continue forever.

The more faithful we are to Christ, the more glorious that moment will be. Spend a few minutes dreaming of that moment, and then live in faith to make that a reality.

● **Cool Down:** Pray an Our Father.

DAY 13

THE BODY AND THE BLOOD

- **Stretch:** Prayers of blessing and adoration.
- **Hydration:** JOHN 6:53–54, 66 | MATTHEW 26:26–28 | 1 CORINTHIANS 11:26–27
- **Reflection:** Could not Christ's word, which can make from nothing what did not exist, change existing things into what they were not before? —*St. Ambrose*

In John 6 we see Jesus arguing with the men of the time. He makes it clear that they need to eat his flesh and drink his blood to have eternal life. He says it over and over again, making such a point of it that many of his disciples leave Him.

It all made sense at the Last Supper. The Second Person of the Trinity, the living Word, in the fullness of his humanity lifted up bread and said, "This is my body." He lifted up the wine and said, "This is my blood." This was the same Word that cried out, "Let there be light," at the beginning of creation (Genesis 1:3; see also John 1:3). When he pointed to his disciples and said, "Do this," they were immediately given power to celebrate what we now call the Eucharist, the real Body and Blood of Jesus Christ, made present in the consecrated bread and wine at Mass.

The Eucharist is the central sacrament of our faith. At Mass we have a chance for the most intimate moment with God on earth as He comes to dwell in us in Holy Communion. It is not just symbolic. It is the Body, Blood, soul, and divinity of Christ.

If we treat the Eucharist as though it were just bread and wine, we sin against Jesus, as Paul said in 1 Corinthians. Ask for God's mercy on all the times you have "casually" received Him. And next time you are at Mass, reflect more deeply on the miracle before you.

Have you heard the phrase "You are what you eat"? At Mass we have a chance to become more like Jesus through the Eucharist. We can also worship the Eucharist outside of Mass, whether He is exposed or in the tabernacle.

● **Cool Down:** Pray an Our Father.

THE HAIL MARY

● Stretch: Prayers of blessing and adoration.

● Hydration: LUKE 1:26–28 | LUKE 1:41–42 | JOHN 19:26–27

● Reflection: The Most High God came down to us in a perfect way through the humble Virgin Mary, without losing anything of his divinity or holiness. It is likewise through Mary that we poor creatures must ascend to almighty God in a perfect manner without having anything to fear. —*St. Louis de Montfort*

On the cross Jesus gave His mother to the apostle John, and by doing so He also gave Mary to the Church. Mary is the most amazing human to ever exist. Who else can claim to be a daughter of the Father, the mother of the Son, and the spouse of the Holy Spirit?

God chose Mary to play an essential role in the story of our salvation. Just as sin came into the world through Eve's *no* to God, salvation came into the world through Mary's *yes*. She is "blessed" not just among women but among all of humanity. We see in Mary the perfect disciple, the perfect humility, the perfect obedience.

The heritage of our Catholic faith is rich with devotions to Mary, our Blessed Mother. But true devotion doesn't end with Mary—it leads us more deeply to Christ. When we pray to Mary, we ask our mother, who knows Jesus more intimately than anyone else in human history, to bring us to her Son. Mary, like all the saints, prays for us. She doesn't have the power of God, nor do we adore her as we do God. The best way to call out to her is through the Hail Mary.

The Hail Mary comes mostly from Scripture. "Hail Mary, full of grace, the Lord is with thee," comes from the angel Gabriel's greeting to Mary in Luke 1:28. "Blessed are you among women, and blessed is the fruit of your womb," is what her cousin Elizabeth exclaimed when she saw her in Luke 1:42. So we begin our prayer by addressing Mary in the same way she was addressed in Scripture. "Holy Mary, Mother of God" acknowledges her role in salvation history. "Mother of God" doesn't mean we think she created God; it clearly says that Mary wasn't just the mother of a human prophet but the mother of God Himself. "Pray for us sinners, now and at the hour of our death." We ask Mary to pray for what we need right now and to prepare us for the time when we take our final breath.

From now on we're going to add the Hail Mary prayer to the workout. But like the Our Father, don't just say the words thoughtlessly. Call out to your mother with your heart. She loves you!

PS: You've just finished the second week of this spiritual workout! Think of a simple way to reward yourself.

● **Cool Down:** Pray an Our Father and a Hail Mary.

FAT-BURNING

● **Stretch:**   Prayers of blessing and adoration.

● **Hydration:**   1 JOHN 1:8–9 | LAMENTATIONS 3:22–23
                   JAMES 5:16

● **Reflection:**   For mercy is an indispensable dimension
                   of love; it is as it were love's second name.
                   —*Blessed John Paul II*

Most people work out to lose weight. That's why fat-burning exercises are so popular. In your spiritual workout you need to burn fat off as well. The fat in our souls is also known as sin.

After you stretch (prayers of blessing and adoration), take a few moments to bring before God any ways that you have sinned against Him. This isn't about making yourself feel bad (though it's important that you regret what you've done). It's about rejoicing in God's mercy, in the fact that He has the power and desire to remove our sins from us "as far as the east is from the west" (Psalm 103:12).

This will also help us in that all-important virtue of humility, which is the foundation of prayer. We come before God sinful, and He restores us through His love. Remember what Jesus said: "Those who are healthy do not need a physician, but the sick do. I have not come to call the righteous to repentance but sinners" (Luke 5:31–32).

So if you're a sinner, then you've come to the right place.

After you bless and adore God, you're going to add a few minutes to say you are sorry for your sins and rejoice in His mercy. Then you'll be in a great place to reflect upon His word in Scripture.

PS: Just like lifting our hands is a great way to bless and adore, kneeling is an appropriate way to show sorrow for our sins.

If you want to read more, check out the *Catechism of the Catholic Church*, 2629–2631.

● **Cool Down:** Pray an Our Father and a Hail Mary.

YOUR ENEMY

- **Stretch:** Prayers of blessing and adoration.
- **Fat-Burning:** Confess your sins to God, and joyfully accept His mercy.
- **Hydration:** EPHESIANS 6:12 | JAMES 4:7 | 1 PETER 5:8–9
- **Reflection:** For God judged it better to bring good out of evil than not to permit any evil to exist. —*St. Augustine*

The devil would have you believe one of two things: that he does not exist, or that he has the power of God.

The devil (also known as Satan or Lucifer) is a fallen angel. Angels, like us, were given a free choice to follow God. The devil and other fallen angels (demons) rebelled. The devil not only hates God, he also hates us, because we are made in the image and likeness of God. He can't fight God, so he tries to destroy us. The best way to hurt a loving father is to kill his children.

Now, before you get too concerned, let's talk about the power of the devil. If you have never given serious thought to the devil's existence (which is his first tactic), then you may start to overestimate his power (his second tactic). In the hierarchy of heaven, God is *way* at the top. About a universe down is Mary, our Blessed Mother, who can crush Satan with her heel. St. Michael the Archangel defeated Satan when he rebelled. So compared to God and the angels and saints, the devil is nothing.

Why does God let the devil exist? A better question is, "Why do we let the devil exist?" We let the devil exist by continuing to rebel against God. Satan tempts us, but *we* choose to sin. The devil can't read our minds (because he's not God), but he can see our weaknesses. God has overcome the snares of the devil, though. When we live in Him, we have no reason to fear.

Our battle is a spiritual one. Things like Ouija boards, tarot cards, and psychics can lure us away from God. If you have been part of those things, get them out of your life. St. Peter tells us to be "sober and vigilant" (1 Peter 5:8). In other words, pay attention! There is a spiritual battle going on all around us. The best way to fight it is on our knees in prayer.

As you pray the Our Father, take some time with the last line of the prayer, "Deliver us from evil." Thank God that He has already won the victory over the devil.

⬤ **Cool Down:** Pray an Our Father and a Hail Mary.

TEMPTATION

Stretch: Prayers of blessing and adoration.

Fat-Burning: Confess your sins to God, and joyfully accept His mercy.

Hydration: 1 CORINTHIANS 10:12–13 | HEBREWS 2:18 JAMES 1:13–15

Reflection: Do not grieve over the temptations you suffer. When the Lord intends to bestow a particular virtue on us, He often permits us first to be tempted by the opposite vice. Therefore, look upon every temptation as an invitation to grow in a particular virtue and a promise by God that you will be successful, if only you stand fast. —*St. Philip Neri*

We must distinguish between temptation and sin. We cannot be free of temptation, but we can avoid sin.

Our holiness is not marked by how little we are tempted but by our actions when we are. Temptation is the first step to sin, but it is not sin itself. Though God allows temptation, it is not He who tempts us. We are tempted by the world around us, by our flesh, and by the devil.

God is not inactive during our temptation. He is always there to help us. He promised that he will never allow us to be tempted beyond our ability to resist it, and He will always give us a way out (see 1 Corinthians 10:13).

Though temptation is something we all bear, we have a responsibility to avoid it as much as we can. We have an obligation to avoid putting ourselves in situations we know to be full of temptation. We need prudence—the use of our moral reason to know what is the right thing to do in each situation. It is "common sense" based in God's truths.

A prudent person avoids tempting situations. If that person is trying not to swear, he or she will avoid music and films that use bad words. If the person struggles with alcohol, he or she won't go into bars.

The bottom line is this: Overcoming temptation begins with choosing not to sin, which is not as simple as it sounds. The truth is that we enjoy sin (otherwise, why would we do it?). For example, God might be calling you to marriage when you will enjoy the gift of sex with your future husband or wife, but the devil offers that gift "right now" with your current boyfriend or girlfriend. The gift is from God, but it is more "stolen" than "given." The shortcuts that sin offers lead only to death, spiritually and even physically.

So what should we do when we are being tempted? *Pray*. The Our Father is a powerful prayer. Another way to fight temptation is to memorize Scripture. (Try 1 Corinthians 10:12–13.) Scripture lets you use God's words of truth against the deceiver.

Pray about the situations in which you put yourself, the ones that lead you to sin. See the connection, and take responsibility to avoid them.

● **Cool Down:** Pray an Our Father and a Hail Mary.

THE MERCY OF GOD

● **Stretch:** Prayers of blessing and adoration.
● **Fat-Burning:** Confess your sins to God, and joyfully accept His mercy.
● **Hydration:** LUKE 15:11–24
● **Reflection:** Do not doubt, do not hesitate, never despair of the mercy of God. —*St. Isidore of Seville*

A father had two sons, the younger of whom wanted his inheritance right away. "I want you to give me the money I'd get from you when you die," he said. Amazingly, the father agreed. So the son took the money and went off to a distant land to "live it up," to party all night long.

The problem with partying all night long is that the night doesn't last forever. Soon the son had wasted all his money, and he became so poor and hungry that he had to work with pigs.

There he was, longing to eat the slop the pigs ate! (Have you ever seen how nasty pig slop is?)

In this pitiful state the son came to his senses. He realized that even the lowliest of his father's servants had it better than he did. So he headed back home, hoping to at least get a decent job.

When he was still a long way off, his father saw him coming, because every day the father had been waiting for his son to come home. Once the father saw his child, he ran toward him. Before the son could even finish what he wanted to say, the father hugged him and welcomed him home. And then the celebration began. It is ironic that this son who left his home to "party" found the best one in his father's house.

God is the Father. We are the son. And every time we repent of our sins, He welcomes us home with open arms. He never gets tired of forgiving us. All we need to do is to turn to Him, and His mercy does the rest.

God's mercy is a gift we cannot earn. All we have to do is receive it with a humble and contrite heart.

There are many things we must do to grow in holiness and faith. But our actions are one-millionth of what we need to be saved and to have a relationship with God. God's free gift of grace covers the rest of it.

Reread the story of the prodigal son, picturing yourself in it. No matter how far you stray, your loving Father is watching and waiting for you to return. Truly, "there is no place like home."

● **Cool Down:** Pray an Our Father and a Hail Mary.

FORGIVING OTHERS

● **Stretch:** Prayers of blessing and adoration.

● **Fat-Burning:** Confess your sins to God, and joyfully accept His mercy.

● **Hydration:** MATTHEW 18:21–35

● **Reflection:** "Do you forgive Alessandro?"

"Yes, of course, Father. Jesus forgave the penitent thief on the Cross and I shall pray that Alessandro may be penitent." *—St. Maria Goretti, on her deathbed, forgiving the man who stabbed her because she wouldn't have sex with him*

Our Christian faith is not just about being forgiven but also about forgiving others. In the Our Father we pray, "Forgive us our trespasses as we forgive those who trespass against us."

Jesus showed us the connection between the mercy we show to others and the mercy we receive.

Since God has shown such mercy to us, we *must* show it to others. The parable that Jesus told Peter shows us God's perspective on why we should forgive others. God paid an *enormous debt* for our sins. Can't we then forgive each other?

Forgiveness is a choice, not a feeling. We might still feel hurt by someone, but we can choose to forgive. That begins healing the wounds we have received.

God knows how hard it is to forgive—He had to die on a cross to forgive us! But through the power of that cross, He gives us the grace to let go of the ways we have been hurt and forgive those who have hurt us. Forgiving others is one of the key ways we experience freedom in Christ.

There is one more important person you must forgive: yourself. Many times we think we've sinned so badly that God can't let us off the hook so simply. But His mercy is simple, and it is open to all hearts that turn to Him.

Think about the people who have hurt you, and forgive them. If you can't, pray for the grace to do so, and talk to someone about it. In your prayers ask God to allow those you have hurt to forgive you. Most importantly, allow yourself to receive the mercy of God.

● **Cool Down:** Pray an Our Father and a Hail Mary.

RECONCILIATION

- **Stretch:** Prayers of blessing and adoration.
- **Fat-Burning:** Confess your sins to God, and joyfully accept His mercy.
- **Hydration:** JOHN 20:21–23 | PSALM 103:11–12
  2 CORINTHIANS 5:18, 20
- **Reflection:** Hide nothing from your confessor.... A sick man can be cured only by revealing his wounds. —*St. Margaret of Cortona*

Many people say, "Do I have to go to confession? I think God forgives me without it." These are just excuses that keep them away from the sacrament. The sacrament of reconciliation is a gift from God, not a punishment.

In baptism we were washed clean of sin, but we were left with our human weaknesses. When we sin, our souls once again become stained. How can we return to our baptismal state of grace? Reconciliation. In that sacrament our souls are again washed clean, and it is as though we have just emerged from the baptismal waters. Though we are baptized only once, we can receive reconciliation time and time again.

In John 20 we see Jesus empowering the apostles with the ability to forgive sins in His name. Today's apostles are our bishops and priests. When they speak the words of absolution, "I forgive you of all of your sins," they are speaking in the person of Christ! Only God can forgive sins, and He gave this ministry of reconciliation to the Church for our benefit. The priest is there to forgive, not condemn. He is there to say the words of Christ: "Your sins are forgiven."

In our walk with Christ, we can perform actions that sever our relationship with Him. These are known as mortal sins. Only through the sacrament of reconciliation can we be restored to His grace. Lesser sins, known as venial sins, can be forgiven through prayer and receiving the Eucharist, but reconciliation brings added grace to those wounds as well. The sacrament of reconciliation heals our souls, and we receive grace and advice to help overcome those sins in the future. Bishops suggest that we receive reconciliation every month to help us live holy lives.

When is the last time you went to reconciliation? Maybe it would be good to look at your schedule and see when you can go again.

PS: You've finished Day 20. Whoa! You're halfway there! And yes, you are also living on a prayer.

● **Cool Down:** Pray an Our Father and a Hail Mary.

RUNNING THE RACE

- **Stretch:** Prayers of blessing and adoration.
- **Fat-Burning:** Confess your sins to God, and joyfully accept His mercy.
- **Hydration:** 1 CORINTHIANS 9:24–27 | 1 TIMOTHY 4:7–9 PROVERBS 5:22–23
- **Reflection:** Let us run with perseverance the race that is set before us, looking to Jesus the pioneer and perfector of our faith. —*Hebrews 12:2*

I knew a guy who ran to school every day—not because he didn't have a ride but because he wanted to be a winning athlete. He watched what he ate, got to bed on time, and worked out every day. He was disciplined, and it paid off. He became a football star and the number-one wrestler in the state.

Webster's dictionary describes *discipline* as "training that develops self-control, character, or efficiency." It means we commit to our goal. It means we make sacrifices to attain that goal. It means we run the race—every step, every day. But we do not run aimlessly. We follow Christ. The word *discipline* comes from the word *disciple*, and we cannot expect to be disciples of Christ without it.

"Train yourself for devotion," writes St. Paul (1 Timothy 4:7). This faith of ours is not just an intellectual exercise; it requires hard work. We must be active. We don't become holy by wishing to be holy.

Anything worth having requires hard work. Every athlete sets goals for himself or herself in order to get better. Someone who can bench 150 pounds will go for 200; somebody who runs a mile in four minutes will try for a time of 3:50.

We can't rest on the gifts that God gives us; we must use them if we want them to grow. So like an athlete, you spiritually work out by praying every day. If you have been faithful to these devotionals, I am confident that you feel stronger in the Lord.

But our race is a marathon, not a sprint. A sprinter puts all of his energies into one quick moment and then collapses at the finish line. A marathon runner, though slower at the start, will outdistance the sprinter. In our run with Christ, distance (or perseverance) is more important than speed. It is better to pray a little bit each day than an hour one day a week.

You've been doing this spiritual workout for three weeks now. Do a spiritual self-check: How are you as a spiritual athlete? What else do you need to do to grow stronger with Christ?

● **Cool Down:** Pray an Our Father and a Hail Mary.

BUILDING MUSCLE

- **Stretch:** Prayers of blessing and adoration.
- **Fat-Burning:** Confess your sins to God, and joyfully accept His mercy.
- **Hydration:** MATTHEW 6:7–8 | 1 TIMOTHY 2:1 | JOB 42:10
- **Reflection:** We can only learn to know ourselves and do what we can—namely, surrender our will and fulfill God's will in us. —*St. Teresa of Avila*

One of the most popular muscle-building exercises is lifting weights. In our spiritual workout we "lift" things too. But we're not lifting weights—we're lifting our needs to God.

Praying for what we need is called the prayer of *petition*. Praying for others is called the prayer of *intercession*. And they are both great things to do after you've been "hydrated" by God's Word.

For some people their entire prayer consists of this. They come to God because they want something, and then they get upset with God because they don't get what they ask for. But Jesus is not Santa Claus or a magical ATM that spits out any amount you ask for. He is a Person, and prayer is a *relationship*. The heart of prayer isn't trying to get what you want but trying to love God (and experience His love) in a deeper way.

So the heart of our prayer of petition must be what Jesus told us to pray in the Our Father: *Your will be done*. We should want what He wants, knowing that His will is "good and pleasing and perfect" (Romans 12:2).

After we pray for His will, we can offer Him the desires of our heart for ourselves and for those we love. Jesus wants us to ask Him for what we need. But we must always remember that our prayer is a request, not a demand. (See, there's the need for *humility* again!) And when we pray, seeking His will above ours, we trust in the words of Jesus, "If you remain in me and my words remain in you, ask for whatever you want and it will be done for you" (John 15:7).

You're doing great! But don't forget that your strength comes from the Holy Spirit, not yourself. So continue to ask the Spirit to lead you deeper in prayer.

If you want to read more, check out the *Catechism of the Catholic Church*, 2632–2636.

- **Muscle-Building:** Pray for God's will, for your needs, and for others.
- **Cool Down:** Pray an Our Father and a Hail Mary.

DAY 23

THE PLEDGE

- **Stretch:** Prayers of blessing and adoration.
- **Fat-Burning:** Confess your sins to God, and joyfully accept His mercy.
- **Hydration:** TOBIT 8:7 | 1 CORINTHIANS 6:18–20
  SIRACH 18:30–32
- **Reflection:** It is well known...that [Mary's] powerful name gives the particular strength necessary to overcome temptations against purity.
  —*St. Alphonsus de Liguori*

I consciously gave my life to Jesus when I was fourteen years old. I didn't know all there was to know about the faith (still don't), but I knew a few important things: I shouldn't steal stuff, I shouldn't lie, I should go to church every Sunday, and I should save sex for marriage. So I made a commitment to stay a virgin until I got married.

Sounds noble, right? Well, in the spirit of full disclosure, I must admit that, at that age, no girl had *even remotely* expressed a desire to sleep with me. I was the freshman in high school that showed up and made you wonder who let the sixth graders in. Girls didn't find me attractive, and I didn't like them much either. (As a fan of D&D and fantasy books, my ideal woman was an elven princess who knew karate and was good with a knife—a standard most thirteen- and fourteen-year-old Catholic schoolgirls didn't live up to.)

By the time I graduated from college, I was dating a wonderful Christian girl. We had even entertained the idea of marriage. We both loved the Lord and prayed together. But we were clearly confused about the chastity thing. We didn't have sex, but we weren't sexually pure either. Then I went to a conference where I heard that chastity was not a restriction—it was a gift! Chastity protects beautiful relationships, while sexual activity confuses and destroys them.

I was thrilled to hear this liberating truth. I filled out a "chastity pledge" card, putting my name and the date on it. I got an extra one for my girlfriend, bought her a copy of the talk on cassette (yes, that's what we used back then), and mailed them to her with great excitement. She also loved the message, and we committed ourselves to a pure and chaste relationship. I was more convinced than ever that she was THE ONE.

Six months later we broke up.

Sexual activity is like a drug, and when we got "sober" we realized that there were things about each other that were downright annoying. I was thankful to realize this, at least in my mind. But my heart was furious. I desired love. I thought she was THE ONE. And that stupid card blew it!

Eighteen months later I was dating another girl, one with bright blue eyes and curly hair. I finally understood with her what it meant to have a chaste relationship. One day, we were praying together when I opened my Bible and the pledge card fell out. Though I had not forgotten my commitment to be chaste, I had forgotten that the card was there. My new girlfriend picked up the card, and she looked as though she was going to cry. She reached in her Bible and pulled out her chastity pledge card. "Look!" she said.

I nodded. She had a pledge card too. Lots of people had them.

She could tell I was missing her point. "Look closer," she said, handing me both cards.

I looked at them. They weren't just both pledge cards, they were the *exact* same card. From the same conference. *On the same date.* When I was in one corner of the room, committing myself to God and my future spouse to stay pure for my marriage, she was in another corner of the room, pledging the same thing.

We were married a year later.

I share this personal story with you to give you hope. God has an amazing plan for your life. No matter what you've done or where you've been, God can get you on the right path to the fullness of life He has planned for you.

- **Muscle-Building:** Pray for God's will, for your needs, and for others.
- **Cool Down:** Pray an Our Father and a Hail Mary.

REST STOP

● **Stretch:** Prayers of blessing and adoration.

● **Fat-Burning:** Confess your sins to God, and joyfully accept His mercy.

● **Hydration:** PSALM 46:11 | PSALM 62:2 | MATTHEW 11:28–30

● **Reflection:** Who except God can give you peace? Has the world ever been able to satisfy the heart? —*St. Gerard Majella*

Do you ever feel so overwhelmed that you have no time for a break?

I know many people who are pulled about by school, activities, homework, work, athletics, and so on. It seems as if they never have time for themselves. They are always heading out to practice or a rehearsal or a job.

Why do we allow ourselves to get so busy? Some of us need to be active in order to feel productive. Others hide behind activities so we won't have to face the pain in our lives. Some of us do it for status: We try to impress people by the amount of stuff we do. Others just get caught up in constant activity; it's almost like a drug.

Maybe we're afraid of silence. We wake up to music blaring, run downstairs and turn on the TV, get in the car and turn on the radio, listen to an iPod during the day, come home and turn on the TV, and then pop on the radio to go to sleep!

What does Psalm 46 tell us today? "Be still and know that I am God." I used to think that I couldn't hear God, but then I realized that I was drowning Him out with the noise of my life. It's not that He wasn't speaking; I just couldn't hear Him above the noise.

Our time with God is a time to be still. We turn off the radio, TV, phone; we free ourselves from distractions to spend a quiet moment with God. God often speaks to us softly. We have to be quiet to hear Him.

When our lives become hurried, the first thing many of us drop is prayer. But if God gave you a "to do" list every day, the first item on it would be "Pray." If Satan had a "to do" list for his demons, the first item on it would be "Keep (insert your name) from praying."

Every athlete needs rest. Why? To relax, rejuvenate, and reenergize. Prayer does that for us. "Come to me, all you who labor and are burdened, and I will give you rest," says our Lord (Matthew 11:28).

Try to spend a minute being still. Turn off any distracting noises. Put aside the cares of the day. Imagine His love showering upon you. Focus on a cross or your favorite picture of Jesus. Be still, and know that He is God.

- **Muscle-Building:** Pray for God's will, for your needs, and for others.
- **Cool Down:** Pray an Our Father and a Hail Mary.

DAY 25

GET UP!

- **Stretch:**   Prayers of blessing and adoration.
- **Fat-Burning:** Confess your sins to God, and joyfully accept His mercy.
- **Hydration:**   ROMANS 7:22–25 | 2 CORINTHIANS 12:9–10 ISAIAH 40:31
- **Reflection:** It is human to fall, but angelic to rise again. —*St. Mary Euphrasia Pelletier*

In running this race, we fall. Sometimes it is a little trip, a stumble. Sometimes we fall flat on our faces. We feel that we are not getting anywhere in our faith, because we continually get caught up in sin. We might make some progress but then feel as if we are back where we started. This can get very frustrating, and it can even make us lose hope.

Don't be discouraged!

St. Paul shared his battle with sin. As holy as he was, he still had problems. That should encourage us: We are not alone in our struggles.

In fact, all Christians struggle with sin until the day they die. Jesus tells us that He came "not...to call the righteous...but sinners" (Luke 5:32). We do not have to be perfect to come to Christ; we come to Christ to be perfected.

Peter and Judas both betrayed Jesus. Peter denied Him three times outside the gates; Judas sold Him out to the Pharisees. Yet one of them founded the Church we believe in, while the other's name went down in history as a traitor. What was the difference between the two?

In their sin they both fell down. When Judas faced despair, he hanged himself. He acknowledged his sin, but he didn't repent of it.

Peter got up again. When Jesus confronted him, he reaffirmed his love. That's what made him a saint. The lesson to be learned from him is this: When you fall, get back up.

Our relationship with Jesus Christ gives us the power to rise again. When we turn to God with a repentant heart, He always helps us up. A man who keeps falling and rising will make more progress than the one who falls and stays down.

Sin is serious. But once we have sinned, the best thing to do is to cry out to God in repentance and let Him pick us up. There is no need to dwell on our sin. His grace is enough to keep us in the race. Meditate on 2 Corinthians 12:9–10.

- **Muscle-Building:** Pray for God's will, for your needs, and for others.
- **Cool Down:** Pray an Our Father and a Hail Mary.

THE HOLY SPIRIT

● **Stretch:** Prayers of blessing and adoration.

● **Fat-Burning:** Confess your sins to God, and joyfully accept His mercy.

● **Hydration:** LUKE 12:11–12 | ACTS 1:8

● **Reflection:** [B]y the sacrament of Confirmation, [the baptized] are more perfectly bound to the Church and are enriched with a special strength of the Holy Spirit. —CCC, *1285, quoting Vatican II, Lumen Gentium, 11*

It was a pretty amazing transformation. One night the disciples were running away in fear from the authorities, and a month later they were preaching Christ in the streets. What happened? The answer: the Holy Spirit. The Holy Spirit is the Third Person of God. Though we often see Him portrayed as a tongue of fire or a dove, He is so much more than that. So how does God the Holy Spirit impact our lives?

The Holy Spirit gives us *power* (see Philippians 4:13). Jesus promised the apostles that they would receive power when the Holy Spirit came, and they sure did. Through the Holy Spirit they healed, cast out demons, and did other miraculous things.

The Holy Spirit gives us *wisdom*. In the Gospel of Luke, Jesus told his disciples not to worry because the Holy Spirit would tell them what to say. When you face tough choices, pray for the Holy Spirit's guidance to know what is right and for the strength to do it.

In baptism we receive the Holy Spirit. He dwells within us, and He is our guide, our comforter, and our friend in this journey to Christ. But baptism is not the final step. In Acts 8 we read of Christians receiving the Holy Spirit in fullness when Peter and John went to them and laid their hands upon them. Today our bishops lay hands upon the baptized for the sacrament of confirmation. In confirmation the gifts you received in baptism become mature. Baptism is the planting of a seed of faith, and confirmation is the blossoming of it.

We can all call upon the Holy Spirit for strength, wisdom, and intimacy with God. Pray the prayer to the Holy Spirit, and spend some time thanking Him for dwelling within you. His presence within you unites you to the life of the Trinity.

Come Holy Spirit,
fill the hearts of your faithful
and kindle in them the fire of your love
Send forth your Spirit, and they shall be created.
And You shall renew the face of the earth.
Let us pray.
O, God,
who by the light of the Holy Spirit
did instruct the hearts of the faithful,
grant that by the same Holy Spirit
we may be truly wise and ever enjoy His consolations.
Through Christ Our Lord. Amen.

- **Muscle-Building:** Pray for God's will, for your needs, and for others.
- **Cool Down:** Pray an Our Father and a Hail Mary.

LIVING ON THE ROCK

● **Stretch:**   Prayers of blessing and adoration.

● **Fat-Burning:** Confess your sins to God, and joyfully accept His mercy.

● **Hydration:**   MATTHEW 16:16–20 | COLOSSIANS 1:17–18

● **Reflection:** The world was created for the sake of the Church. —*St. Justin and other early Christians, as quoted in* CCC, 760

What is the Church? Just a collection of people who believe the same things? An institution of rules and regulations? Many don't believe in "organized" religion. Others say the Church has no real authority because men, not God, created it. The Bible tells us otherwise. In Matthew we see Jesus planning a Church and naming Peter as the head (16:18).

Living in a democracy as we do, the way the Church works seems odd or unfair to us. We don't vote for our popes. The Church doesn't ask our opinion on various topics. Who is the Church to tell us what to do? The Church is ordained by God to care for His people and lead us to heaven. Jesus established the Church, and the Holy Spirit protects and guides her.

In each of us there is a visible and invisible reality: We have human bodies, but we also have souls, which cannot be seen. So too, outwardly the Church is a hierarchy of people, but invisibly she is the Mystical Body of Christ and Jesus is made present through her. What she teaches is what God commands. What else did Jesus mean when He told Peter, "What you bind on earth is bound in heaven, and what you unbind on earth is unbound in heaven"?

Jesus founded the Church and established it through Peter, "and the gates of the netherworld shall not prevail against it" (Matthew 16:18). Some only want to follow Scripture, but it was the Church that gathered Scripture together and validated its use! We believe in what the apostles passed down in writing (Scripture), what passed down through their teaching (Tradition), and the authority of the pope and bishops who guide us today (the Magisterium).

In the Church we are united (*one*). In the Church we receive the sacraments, which make us *holy*. The Church is open to everyone, both genders and every race (*catholic*). And in the Church we are united to the apostles and the heritage of faith lived through the saints (*apostolic*). One. Holy. Catholic. Apostolic. Sound familiar?

You are not on your own. You are part of something much, much bigger. Did you know there are over a billion Catholics in the world? That's one out of seven people. The Church's history is *your* history. The Church's family is *your* family. Take some time to reflect on what it means to be a part of the Church, and thank Jesus that He didn't leave us on our own.

- **Muscle-Building:** Pray for God's will, for your needs, and for others.
- **Cool Down:** Pray an Our Father and a Hail Mary.

Building a Healthy Heart

- **Stretch:** Prayers of blessing and adoration.
- **Fat-Burning:** Confess your sins to God, and joyfully accept His mercy.
- **Hydration:** Psalm 28:7 | Psalm 138:1–2
- **Reflection:** No duty is more urgent than that of returning thanks. —*St. Ambrose*

Good physical workouts should strengthen the heart. Spiritual workouts should do that too.

The Bible talks about "the heart" over a thousand times! But Scripture isn't talking about the physical organ that pumps blood in our chest. It is referring to our hidden center, the dwelling place where we live.

One great way to strengthen our hearts is the prayer of thanksgiving and praise. Though they sound like the same thing, there is an importance difference: Thanksgiving is rejoicing because of *what God has done*; praise gives God glory because of *who He is*. Make sure to do both!

I find that, even when I'm not in a thankful mood, there is always reason to give God praise. He is glorious whether or not I'm having a "good day." And as I focus on praising Him for who He is, I become more aware of all the amazing things He has done, and then I am more thankful.

A great way to end your workout each day is to spend time thanking God for what He's done and praising God for who He is. By doing so you let God do "heart surgery": "I will give you a new heart, and a new spirit I will put within you. I will remove the heart of stone from your flesh and give you a heart of flesh" (Ezekiel 36:26).

If you want to read more, check out the *Catechism of the Catholic Church*, 2563 and 2637–2643.

And here's something to thank God for: You've made it through four weeks of the spiritual workout! Do something to celebrate!

- **Muscle-Building:** Pray for God's will, for your needs, and for others.
- **Cardiovascular:** Thank Him for what He's done, and praise Him for who He is.
- **Cool Down:** Pray an Our Father and a Hail Mary.

DAY 29

FASTING

● **Stretch:** Prayers of blessing and adoration.
● **Fat-Burning:** Confess your sins to God, and joyfully accept His mercy.
● **Hydration:** MATTHEW 6:17–18 | SIRACH 37:28–30
● **Reflection:** A man who governs his passions is master of his world. We must either command them or be enslaved by them. It is better to be a hammer than an anvil. —*St. Dominic*

Fasting is a form of prayer. Isn't it interesting that Jesus said, "*When* you fast" instead of "*If* you fast"? Fasting is the sacrifice or giving up of things in order to draw closer to God. As Catholics there are many times when we are called to fast together. We fast during the forty days of Lent. We also fast every Friday before Easter and after Pentecost. But what's the point?

We fast to detach ourselves from the stuff of this earth so that we can cling more tightly to heaven. We will never grow in holiness if we don't understand this simple truth: Not all pleasure is good, and not all pain is bad. Things that feel great can kill. Things that cause some pain or discomfort can be good in the long run. Athletes know this. So should we.

This world encourages us to eat all we want, drink all we want, watch all we want, and play all we want. This is known as gluttony—being enslaved to the desires of our bodies. If our stomachs grumble, we immediately feed them. If we want something, we buy it immediately. Materialism is attachment to things in this life: clothing, TVs, computers, cars, music, etc. Lust is the attempt to satiate our sexual desires with pornography, fantasies, sexual activity, etc. Debauchery is eating and drinking as much as we can; it can include drunkenness and drug usage. We fall into sin when we can't say no to our bodies.

And that's why we fast. Fasting builds up the virtue of temperance or moderation. Temperance helps us keep things in order; it keeps us from overindulging. Fasting draws us closer to God. You don't need to fast only from food. We can offer

Jesus any suffering we feel and share in his suffering for us. You can fast from TV, radio, the phone, or anything else you may be attached to. Don't get carried away, though. The goal is not to kill ourselves but to detach ourselves!

Think of what you can give up this Friday, and join in the prayerful fast of the Church. You don't have to do the same thing each week. Maybe one Friday you give up TV, another Friday the Internet, another meat, another candy, and so on. Or you can try to do something special instead—extra prayer or helping someone, for example.

Are you in control of your desires, or are your desires in control of you? The best way to get control is by making fasting a regular part of your spiritual life.

- **Muscle-Building:** Pray for God's will, for your needs, and for others.
- **Cardiovascular:** Thank Him for what He's done, and praise Him for who He is.
- **Cool Down:** Pray an Our Father and a Hail Mary.

THE SAINT WHO NEVER WAS

●**Stretch:**   Prayers of blessing and adoration.

●**Fat-Burning:** Confess your sins to God, and joyfully accept His mercy.

●**Hydration:** MATTHEW 19:16–22 | MARK 10:17-22

●**Reflection:** It is not difficult to see how today's world, despite its beauty and grandeur, despite the conquests of science and technology, despite the refined and abundant material goods that it offers, is yearning for more truth, for more love, for more joy. And all of this is found in Christ and in his way of life. —*Blessed Pope John Paul II*

Today is not the feast day of St. Reuben, Apostle.

That's because in the first century AD, Reuben was not beheaded by the Gauls after boldly proclaiming Christ and causing many to believe in Him. Reuben did not famously say before he died, "Since I have given everything else to my Lord, why not also give my life?"

Reuben was not known to be filled with the power of the Holy Spirit. He never earned the nickname "St. Reuben the Blameless" because he had lived out all of the commandments from his youth. Reuben was not picked as the apostle to replace Judas. He was not even in the drawing, because he was not someone who had followed Jesus from the beginning.

When the apostles and the seventy-two gathered together in prayer after Christ ascended into heaven, Reuben was not there. Nor did Christ appear to him after His resurrection and invite him to touch His hands and His side. Was he even in Jerusalem during that Holy Week? We will never know.

You have not heard of St. Reuben because the Church never canonized him. Even the name "Reuben" is fictitious.

So what *do* we know of him? He was young. He had been a faithful Jew, following all the commandments from when he was a child. We know that when he talked to Jesus, Jesus looked at him with love (see Mark 10:21). We also know that he was wealthy. His fine garments distinguished him from the crowd and certainly from the other followers of Christ. When he was invited to join them, did he stare at the disciples' dirty clothes, their tired expressions, their gaunt faces? Did he think of the good food and good rest he enjoyed in the comfort of his own dwelling and prefer it to the hours of long travel and poor shelter he would face by joining Jesus on the road?

> Jesus said to him, "If you wish to be perfect, go, sell what you have and give to the poor, and you will have treasure in heaven. Then come, follow me."
>
> When the young man heard this statement, he went away sad, for he had many possessions. (Matthew 19:21–22)

We do not know what he could have become. We only know how he felt: *sad*. Shrouded in anonymity for the rest of time, all that is remembered of him is the regrettable decision he made and a shallow description of what he looked like: "rich," "young," and "man."

Don't let this happen to you. What is holding you back from being a disciple of Christ?

- **Muscle-Building:** Pray for God's will, for your needs, and for others.
- **Cardiovascular:** Thank Him for what He's done, and praise Him for who He is.
- **Cool Down:** Pray an Our Father and a Hail Mary.

FELLOWSHIP

● **Stretch:** Prayers of blessing and adoration.

● **Fat-Burning:** Confess your sins to God, and joyfully accept His mercy.

● **Hydration:** MATTHEW 18:20 | ECCLESIASTES 4:9–10 HEBREWS 12:1

● **Reflection:** Fly from bad companions as from the bite of a poisonous snake. If you keep good companions, I can assure you that you will one day rejoice with the blessed in Heaven; whereas if you keep with those who are bad, you will become bad yourself, and you will be in danger of losing your soul. —*St. John Bosco*

Many people adopt the attitude, "It's just me and Jesus!" I used to think that way, until I realized that my youth leader was a big part of my spiritual journey. Then I thought it was just me, Jesus, and my youth leader. Then I reflected on how important my parents were in supporting my faith and how my parish priest had encouraged me since I was young. So then it was just me, Jesus, my youth leader, my parish priest, and my parents. But what about my teachers, my grandmother, and my sister who first took me to youth group? Finally I realized that it never was just "me and Jesus." My decision to follow Christ was not an isolated moment.

This is not a journey for lone rangers. As a family now, we are called to fellowship. Fellowship is like friendship, only deeper. We are united not only by hobbies and personalities but by Jesus Christ Himself. He has given His life for us, and He has given us to each other. Fellowship with other Christians helps us overcome sin. This is known as accountability. We can watch each other's back and encourage each other to holiness. By joining together in fellowship, Jesus becomes more present than if we were on our own. He lives among us when we gather in his name. This happens not only at Mass but also at youth group meetings, in prayer over a meal with your family, and with your friends at school.

Just as spending time with Christians can bring us closer to Christ, we have to be careful of spending lots of time with people who may pull us away from Him. The people you hang out with can greatly affect your spiritual life. Maybe you gave your life to Christ on a retreat or conference, only to go home to a group of friends who have no love for God. You think you can evangelize your friends, but more often than not, they "devangelize" you, especially if you're just getting started in your faith. If you want to survive in Christ, you have to hang out with those who follow Him.

- If you don't like hanging out with other Christians, you're in trouble. Heaven is full of them!
- Think about all of the people who have drawn you to Christ, and thank God for them.
- Pray for your friends who are trying to follow Christ, and pledge to do so every day.

• Find a "prayer partner" who will pray for your needs and whom you can pray for.

• Reflect on your relationships: Do they lead you closer to Christ, or do they pull you away?

- **Muscle-Building:** Pray for God's will, for your needs, and for others.

- **Cardiovascular:** Thank Him for what He's done, and praise Him for who He is.

- **Cool Down:** Pray an Our Father and a Hail Mary.

DAY 32

REAL LOVE

- **Stretch:** Prayers of blessing and adoration.
- **Fat-Burning:** Confess your sins to God, and joyfully accept His mercy.
- **Hydration:** JOHN 15:12–13 | 1 CORINTHIANS 13:4–8 1 JOHN 4:7–8
- **Reflection:** At the end of our life, we shall be judged by love. —*St. John of the Cross*

Love, like faith, is not an intellectual thing. It is active. It is also the greatest virtue that we can possess.

Our language has only one word for love. The language Scripture was written in had four. The greatest love of all was called agape [ah-gah-pay]. It was a total self-giving to another. This agape love is what Christ showed us on the cross—and what He commands us to give to each other.

Agape love is an act of the will. It is a choice, a decision. There is nothing especially virtuous about "falling in love" with someone (in an emotional sense). But choosing to love someone is what makes you a Christian. Jesus said, "If you love only those people who love you, will God reward you for that?" (see Matthew 5:46). It is easy to be nice to people who are nice to us, to love those who love us. The challenge of Christianity is to love the unlovable. But how can you love someone you hate? The agape love that Jesus calls us to is not just emotional. The virtue of love (also known as charity) is a decision to give of ourselves to another. We are called to love all people, even people whom we tend to avoid.

Without love everything we do is meaningless. Love gives real purpose to our actions and also the power to perform them, no matter how great the pain. Think of all the mothers who have endured the pain of childbirth out of love for their children and the soldiers who have died out of love for their country. The greatest example is Christ's dying on the cross for us.

Reflect on 1 Corinthians 13:4–8. Go over each description of love, and think of the opposite (kind vs. mean and so on) to find out what love isn't. Do you act in love? If you inserted your name every time the passage says "love," would that describe you? If not, what do you need to work on?

- **Muscle-Building:** Pray for God's will, for your needs, and for others.
- **Cardiovascular:** Thank Him for what He's done, and praise Him for who He is.
- **Cool Down:** Pray an Our Father and a Hail Mary.

YOU ARE THE ONLY YOU THERE IS

- **Stretch:** Prayers of blessing and adoration.
- **Fat-Burning:** Confess your sins to God, and joyfully accept His mercy.
- **Hydration:** PSALM 139:13–14 | ROMANS 12:2 | 1 JOHN 2:17
- **Reflection:** To be in heaven is "to be with Christ." The elect live "in Christ," but they retain, or rather find, their true identity, their own name. —CCC, *1025, quoting Philippians 1:23; see John 14:3; 1 Thessalonians 4:17*

Jesus calls us to be in the world, but we must never forget that this world is not our final home. Though we are called to be *in* the world, we are not called to be *of* the world. We are not supposed to become "worldly" beings. St. Paul warns us,

"Do not conform yourselves to this age but be transformed by the renewal of your mind" (Romans 12:2). Simply put, he is challenging us to let God, not the world, shape the way we think. The world sends us conflicting messages. It says you should be yourself, but then it tells you how to live. "Be an individual...but wear these clothes we're trying to sell you and all your friends." In truth the world wants us all to be the same.

Only in following God can we discover who we really are. Being holy doesn't make us cookie-cutter replicas of each other. Just look at the saints to see how wonderfully unique we can be while still being united in faith.

When St. John tells us not to "love the world," he is not talking about disrespecting the earth. He's talking about not loving the things of this world more than we love God. The possessions, popularity, and power we gain on earth will all pass away. We spend so much time trying to get them! We must instead work to gain the everlasting treasures of our God and our faith.

Pray about what you are "attached" to in this world, and ask God to release you of those attachments. Pray to receive an eternal perspective, so that your focus will be on everlasting goals. Ask God to help you see yourself as He sees you, for you are "fearfully and wonderfully made."

- **Muscle-Building:** Pray for God's will, for your needs, and for others.
- **Cardiovascular:** Thank Him for what He's done, and praise Him for who He is.
- **Cool Down:** Pray an Our Father and a Hail Mary.

OBEDIENCE

● **Stretch:** Prayers of blessing and adoration.

● **Fat-Burning:** Confess your sins to God, and joyfully accept His mercy.

● **Hydration:** ROMANS 13:1–3 | EPHESIANS 6:1–3

● **Reflection:** Obedience is so great a virtue that Our Lord willed to lead his whole life in obedience. He said so many times that he had come not "to do his own will." —*St. Francis de Sales*

We are called to be obedient to our Church and its teachings. We are also called to be obedient to earthly authorities, as long as they don't ask us to sin.

At the time Paul was writing to the Christians in Rome, the Christians decided to stop paying taxes. They figured that since they were now obedient to Christ, they didn't have to obey Roman law. Paul sternly corrected them. Even though the authorities weren't Christian, they were still appointed by God.

The same is true with our parents. The fourth commandment God gave Moses is "Honor your father and your mother" (Exodus 20:12; see Ephesians 6:2–3). When we rebel against our parents, we are rebelling against God.

Paul tells us an easy way of dealing with authorities so that they don't bug you: Obey them. People who don't speed don't worry about cops pulling them over. Kids who honestly tell their parents where they will be that night never worry about getting caught in the wrong place.

We sometimes think that those who rebel are strong and those who follow are weak. A good friend of mine is a Navy Seal. He's one of the strongest guys I know, both physically and spiritually. Guess what? He spends his life following orders. His obedience allows him to work perfectly with a team.

As a follower of Jesus Christ, you are part of a team. But that means you've got to *listen* to the people whom God has put in authority over you.

- **Muscle-Building:** Pray for God's will, for your needs, and for others.
- **Cardiovascular:** Thank Him for what He's done, and praise Him for who He is.
- **Cool Down:** Pray an Our Father and a Hail Mary.

WITNESSING

- **Stretch:**   Prayers of blessing and adoration.
- **Fat-Burning:** Confess your sins to God, and joyfully accept His mercy.
- **Hydration:**   1 PETER 3:15–16 | ROMANS 1:16 | ACTS 1:8
- **Reflection:** Here lies the test of truth, the touchstone of evangelization: it is unthinkable that a person should accept the Word and give himself to the kingdom without becoming a person who bears witness to it and proclaims it in his turn.
  —*Pope Paul VI*

Something that is common to all humanity: We communicate things we get excited about. That might be a favorite sports team, a great book we just read, or an amazing movie we saw. It might be advice on what to eat or what to wear. Perhaps it's a new app we just downloaded or a song that really moves us.

The bottom line is that when we get excited about something, we instinctively tell others about it.

And yet there are many people who seem enthusiastic about their faith but don't share it with others. They are comfortable talking about Jesus in church but are silent when they get home or go to school or work. Why? Why is it more comfortable to talk about a two-hour movie than about the Lord and Savior of our souls? Here are some thoughts:

We don't want to seem "pushy." There is a popular notion that talking about your faith is like "shoving the Bible down someone's throat." But that's not what we're called to do. If we're excited about our faith, we should talk about it. Blessed John Paul II says it this way: "The Church, and every individual Christian within her, may not keep hidden or monopolize this newness and richness which has been received from God's bounty in order to be communicated to all mankind."

We don't know what to say. You don't need a degree in theology or know all the answers to talk about your faith. How has Jesus made a difference in your life? That's something that people can't argue with.

We're afraid of what people might think of us. This is probably the biggest reason of all and one that takes a lot of honesty and humility to admit. Sharing your faith won't win any popularity contests. If your main motivation in life is to get people to like you, you're in the wrong Church. But if your desire is to help people by introducing them to a loving God who cares for them infinitely more than they could ever comprehend, you're in the right place.

Yes, some people will reject you because of your beliefs, but others will be tremendously blessed by them.

You've been doing this spiritual workout for five weeks now. It's time to let people know what God is doing in your life! What holds you back? What can you do to better proclaim Christ in your actions and your words?

- **Muscle-Building:** Pray for God's will, for your needs, and for others.
- **Cardiovascular:** Thank Him for what He's done, and praise Him for who He is.
- **Cool Down:** Pray an Our Father and a Hail Mary.

BE NOT AFRAID

- **Stretch:** Prayers of blessing and adoration.
- **Fat-Burning:** Confess your sins to God, and joyfully accept His mercy.
- **Hydration:** MATTHEW 10:28–31 | ROMANS 8:31, 37
  2 TIMOTHY 1:7
- **Reflection:** Fear is a greater evil than the evil itself. —*St. Francis de Sales*

If there is anything we need in this world, it is the virtue of fortitude. Another word for *fortitude* is *courage.* Like all of the virtues, we can grow in fortitude only when we are challenged.

Being courageous does not mean that we do not fear. It means that we overcome fear by God's grace. We never have the chance to show courage if we are never afraid! St. Paul wrote, "If God is for us, who can be against us?" (Romans 8:31). Ridicule, abuse, and isolation are all things that Jesus had to suffer while on earth. If we live as Jesus did, we might suffer the same way. There are still many places in this world where Christians are killed because of their faith.

The real definition of *fortitude* is "the willingness to die in battle." If we go into a battle ready to die, then we have no reason to fear. It is only when we try to hold on to this life that we lose it. The virtue of fortitude allows us to "let go and let God." A common phrase of Jesus in the Gospels is "Be not afraid." Pope John Paul II reminded us of this again and again. He said at his installation, "Do not be afraid. Open wide the doors for Christ!"

Do you have fears that paralyze you or keep you from living out God's will? If so, offer them to the Lord. The power of God has parted the sea, overcome armies, cured illnesses, raised the dead to life, and conquered death.

What would your life look like if you weren't afraid? Pray for the grace to overcome your fears and trust in the Lord. Then you can live your faith and share it boldly.

- **Muscle-Building:** Pray for God's will, for your needs, and for others.
- **Cardiovascular:** Thank Him for what He's done, and praise Him for who He is.
- **Cool Down:** Pray an Our Father and a Hail Mary.

HUMILITY

● **Stretch:** Prayers of blessing and adoration.

● **Fat-Burning:** Confess your sins to God, and joyfully accept His mercy.

● **Hydration:** LUKE 18:9–14 | 1 PETER 5:5–7 | JAMES 1:16–17

● **Reflection:** That which man is before God, that is what he is and nothing else. —*St. Francis of Assisi*

The *Catechism* tells us that *"humility* is the foundation of prayer" (CCC, 2559). It defines humility as "the virtue by which a Christian acknowledges that God is the author of all good." That's a fascinating definition, so different from how the culture often defines humility. Look up *humble* in the dictionary, and you'll find "not proud," "insignificant," and "lowly." Those describe what humility *looks* like, but not what it *is*.

Humility is acknowledging the power of God in comparison to the smallness of ourselves. Humility is not beating ourselves up or making ourselves seem like something less than we actually are. Humility is truth.

For example, I do many concerts, and sometimes people come up to me afterward and say, "You have a great voice!" *False* humility would have me respond, "No, I don't. My voice is horrible. I'm sorry you had to listen to it." *Real* humility has me respond, "Thank you! I'm very grateful that God has blessed me with my voice, and I'm happy you were blessed by it, too." To deny that God has given me a gift would be an insult to God. It would also be an insult to God to take personal credit for something He has given me. The right balance is to be grateful for the gift and give God the credit. Because that's the truth. And humility is truth.

The world tells us that we have value because of what we *do*. God tells us that we have value in who we *are*. We are made in *His* image and likeness. He is God; we are not. Abandoning ourselves to that beautiful truth gives us freedom, peace, and a grateful heart.

- **Muscle-Building:** Pray for God's will, for your needs, and for others.
- **Cardiovascular:** Thank Him for what He's done, and praise Him for who He is.
- **Cool Down:** Pray an Our Father and a Hail Mary.

WORKS OF MERCY

Stretch: Prayers of blessing and adoration.

Fat-Burning: Confess your sins to God, and joyfully accept His mercy.

Hydration: MATTHEW 25:37–40 | JAMES 2:5–7

Reflection: We have to become increasingly aware that the poor are the hope of humanity, for we will be judged by how we have treated the poor. We will have to face this reality when we are summoned before the throne of God: 'I was hungry. I was naked. I was homeless. And whatever you did to the least of my brethren, you did it to me.' When we recognize that our suffering neighbor is the image of God Himself, and when we understand the consequences of that truth, poverty will no longer exist.
—*Blessed Mother Teresa of Calcutta*

Justice is the virtue that calls us to give people their due. We see justice at work when we feed the hungry, clothe the naked, and visit the sick.

On the face of every needy person is a story. Some of the stories are not pleasant. Some of the stories might even make you think, "This person deserves it." But does anybody deserve to be hungry, poor, or naked? Jesus tells us to reach out to these people. He also tells us to visit prisoners. There is no one "too sinful" for God. His mercy is for us all, and we must extend that mercy to each other.

The easiest way to grow in justice is this: Treat others as you would treat Jesus. He told us that whatever we do for others we do for Him (see Matthew 25:40). What an opportunity!

There is so much poverty, sickness, and imprisonment in the world that it can be overwhelming. Start small. Mother Teresa once said, "If you can't feed a hundred people, then just feed one."

If you are blessed with money, you could sponsor a needy child. If you are blessed with possessions, give some of the things you don't use to the local homeless shelter. If you are blessed with time, spend some of it visiting an elderly person who feels abandoned, or volunteer at a soup kitchen, a pregnancy clinic, or some other charity. Start small, but *do something*.

As a professor, I know that students pay extra attention when I teach something and say, "This will be on the final exam." Well, that's exactly what Jesus says to us in Matthew 25. He tells us how he will separate the righteous from the unrighteous. The righteous will be the ones who fed the hungry, welcomed the stranger, and clothed the naked. The unrighteous did not.

So, are you paying attention? What can you do to be ready for the final test?

- **Muscle-Building:** Pray for God's will, for your needs, and for others.
- **Cardiovascular:** Thank Him for what He's done, and praise Him for who He is.
- **Cool Down:** Pray an Our Father and a Hail Mary.

A DIFFERENT KIND OF LOVE

- **Stretch:** Prayers of blessing and adoration.
- **Fat-Burning:** Confess your sins to God, and joyfully accept His mercy.
- **Hydration:** ROMANS 8:38–39 | SONG OF SONGS 8:6–7 JOHN 15:9
- **Reflection:** Love takes up where knowledge leaves off. —*St. Thomas Aquinas*

Jesus loves you.

No, really. He *loves* you. He's not just interested in you or somewhat attracted to you. He's obsessed with you, like a jealous lover. If that makes you feel a little bit uncomfortable, I think that's OK. Sadly, our relationship with God is not evenly balanced. We say we love God, but it's always in varying degrees and never as much as He loves us.

In my life I'm really focused on God—when I'm in prayer.

Outside of prayer I occasionally think of Him. I wish I could say He was always on my mind. But that wouldn't be honest. Many times I'm thinking of music, the latest superhero movie, or *Doctor Who*.

But Jesus is *always* thinking about me. I sometimes think He must be disappointed that I don't think about Him as much as He thinks about me. I once dated a girl who was *crazy* about me—but I didn't feel at all the same. It was awkward. Then there was another girl who I was *certain* was my soul mate, the one I was made for. But she didn't feel the same. Her boyfriend didn't like the idea either.

In human relationships, if one person is more in love than the other, it can kill the relationship. Thankfully, our relationship with God is not purely a human relationship. Jesus *loves* you not only in a human way but also in a divine way. Human love is just a reflection of the unceasing, unquenchable, and unchanging love of God.

When you pray today, take some quiet time to rest in that love. Don't think about it, don't analyze it. Just accept it. That's what He wants us to do at every moment of our lives.

- **Muscle-Building:** Pray for God's will, for your needs, and for others.
- **Cardiovascular:** Thank Him for what He's done, and praise Him for who He is.
- **Cool Down:** Pray an Our Father and a Hail Mary.

KEEP GOING!

You did it!

My hope for these past forty days was to establish a habit of daily prayer in your life so that you could eventually do it on your own. And now that time has come.

Let's recap what makes a good spiritual workout:

- **Stretch:** Start by blessing God, let Him bless you, and have a moment of adoration.
- **Fat-burning:** Examine the actions of your life, and confess your sins before God. Rejoice in His mercy!
- **Hydration:** This is where you drink of the "living water" of Christ. My suggestion is to start reading the Gospel of Luke, then move on to the other Gospels. The Gospels are the heart of all the Scriptures. They are the story of Jesus Christ, God who became man to save us from our sins.

Read the Gospels, maybe a section or a chapter at a time. Imagine yourself there. Hear the words that Jesus spoke. See the amazing things He did. Feel the wounds in His hands and side, and know that He is God.

- **Muscle-building:** "Lift" up your intercessions to God, always with the main request, "Let your will be done."
- **Cardiovascular:** End by thanking God for what He's done and praising God for who He is!

All these forms of prayer are described in the *Catechism*, 2623–2649. But if you really want to know more about how to pray, you should read the whole fourth section of the *Catechism*, which is titled "Christian Prayer." It's short and beautiful and one of the best things you can read about prayer. (If you don't own a *Catechism*, you can find plenty of free versions online.)

Thanks for accepting the challenge of this spiritual workout. I pray that you will continue to grow stronger in your love for Jesus Christ.

- **Stretch:** Prayers of blessing and adoration.
- **Fat-Burning:** Confess your sins to God, and joyfully accept His mercy.
- **Hydration:** Luke 1:1–25 (Tomorrow read Luke 1:26–38, and so on.)
- **Muscle-Building:** Pray for God's will, for your needs, and for others.
- **Cardiovascular:** Thank Him for what He's done, and praise Him for who He is.
- **Cool Down:** Pray an Our Father and a Hail Mary.

Make sure you do something exciting today to celebrate completing *A 40-Day Spiritual Workout for Catholics*! Great job!

NOTES

Introduction

Thérèse of Lisieux, *Manuscrits autobiographiques*, C 25r, as quoted in the *Catechism of the Catholic Church* (CCC), 2558.

Day 1

Attributed to St. Augustine, bishop of Hippo.

Day 3

St. Rose of Lima, as quoted in *CCC*, 618, citing P. Hansen, *Vita mirabilis* (Louvain: n.p., 1668).

Day 4

C.S. Lewis, *Mere Christianity* (London: Collins, 1952), pp. 54–56.

Day 5

St. Louis De Montfort, *The Secret of the Rosary* (Rockford, Ill.: Tan, 1970), p. 120.

Day 6

St. Thomas Aquinas, *Summa Theologiae* II-II, 83, 9, as quoted in *CCC*, 2763.

Day 8

Third Council of Baltimore, *Baltimore Catechism* (1891), question 6 in lesson 1 of parts 1 and 2.

Augustine, *Confessions*, bk. 1, chap. 1, in *Corpus Scriptorum Ecclesiasticorum Latinorum* (Vienna: n.p., 1866).

Day 9

Pope John Paul II, Homily at 17th World Youth Day, Toronto, Ontario, July 28, 2002. Available at www.vatican.va.

Day 11

St. Augustine of Hippo, *Sermones* 4.1.1.

Day 12

Josemaría Escrivá, *The Way,* #139 (Manila: Sinag-Tala, 1982), p. 35.

Day 13

St. Ambrose, *De mysteriis* 9, 50; 52: *Patrologia Latina* 16, 405–407, as quoted in *CCC*, 1375.

Day 14

St. Louis de Montfort, *True Devotion to the Blessed Virgin Mary,* Translated by Frederick William Faber (Bay Shore, N.Y.: Montfort Fathers, 1941), p. 157.

Day 15

Pope John Paul II, *Dives in Misericordia, 5,* November 30, 1980. Available at www.vatican.va.

Day 16

St. Augustine, *Enchiridion on Faith, Hope, and Love,* 27. Translated by Albert C. Outler. Available at www.tertullian.org.

Day 17

Attributed to St. Philip Neri. Available at www.ewtn.com.

Day 18

Attributed to St. Isidore of Seville. Available at www.ewtn.com.

Day 19

Alexander Gits, *A Modern Virgin Martyr: St. Maria Goretti.* Available at catholicpamphlets.net.

Day 20

St. Margaret of Cortona, quoted in Timothy Michael Dolan, *Priests for the Third Millennium* (Huntington, Ind.: Our Sunday Visitor, 2000), p. 108.

Day 22

St. Teresa of Avila, "The Way of Perfection," in *The Complete Works,* Volume Two, (New York: Continuum, 2002), p. 139.

Day 23

St. Alphonsus de Liguori, "The Holy Name of Mary: The Power of Her Name," *Our Lady of the Rosary Library.* Available at www.olrl.org.

Day 24

Attributed to St. Gerard Majella. Available at Saints.SQPN.com.

Day 25

Attributed to St. Mary Euphrasia Pelletier. Available at Saints. SQPN.com.

Day 28

Attributed to St. Ambrose of Milan.

Day 29

Attributed to St. Dominic Guzman. Available at Saints.SQPN.com.

Day 30

Pope John Paul II, homily at the Boston Common, October 1, 1979. Available at www.vatican.va.

Day 31

Attributed to St. John Bosco. Available at Saints.SQPN.com.

Day 32

St. John of the Cross, quoted by Pope Benedict XVI, Address to Members of the Italian Voluntary Service Organizations, February 10, 2007. Available at www.vatican.va, and reported by Catholic News Service, February 12, 2007.

Day 34

St. Francis de Sales, "A Talk on Obedience to the Visitation Sisters," *The Second Conference*. Available at www.oblates.org.

Day 35

Pope Paul VI, *Evangelii Nuntiandi*, 24, Apostolic Exhortation, December 8, 1975. Available at www.vatican.va.

John Paul II, *Redemptoris Missio,* 11, Encyclical on the Permanent Validity of the Church's Missionary Mandate, December 7, 1990. Available at www.vatican.va.

Day 36

St. Francis de Sales, as quoted by Elizabeth Stopp, *Francis de Sales: Selected Letters* (London: Faber and Faber, 1960), p. 125.

Pope John Paul II, homily at his installation, October 22, 1978. Available at www.vatican.va.

Day 37

St. Francis of Assisi, "Ammonizioni," 19, *Fonti Francescane*, 169, as quoted by Raniero Cantalamessa, "Blessed Are the Pure in Heart," first Lenten sermon, 2007. Available at www.ewtn.com.

Day 38

Blessed Mother Teresa of Calcutta, *No Greater Love* (Novato, Calif.: New World Library, 1997), p. 103.

Day 39

St. Thomas Aquinas, *Summa Theologiae,* II-II, q. 27, a. 4, ad 1.

About the Author

Bob Rice desires to share the love of God using every talent God has blessed him with. He's an internationally known speaker who creatively blends humor and drama in passionate proclamations of the gospel. He is a singer, songwriter, and worship leader who has released ten CDs and who plays to over ten thousand people each year. And he writes: scripts for short films, articles on catechesis and youth ministry, a novel about St. Peter titled *Between the Savior and the Sea*, and a popular blog that deals with the intersection of Catholicism and culture.

Bob teaches catechetics at Franciscan University of Steubenville in Ohio. He lives in Steubenville with his wife, Jennifer, and their six beautiful children.

Small children trust Bob, and woodland creatures eat from his hand. Yes, he's that good. You can keep up with him at bob-rice. com.